You Have to Fucking Eat

by Adam Mansbach

illustrated by Owen Brozman

CANONGATE
Edinburgh · London

Published by Canongate Books in 2014

1

Words © 2014 Adam Mansbach
Illustrations © 2014 Owen Brozman

First published in Great Britain in 2014 by Canongate Books Ltd, 14 High Street, Edinburgh, EH1 1TE

First published in the USA by Akashic Books, 232 Third St., Suite A115, Brooklyn, NY 11215

www.canongate.tv

ISBN: 978 1 78211 636 3

Printed and bound in Slovenia by GPS

Adam Mansbach is the author of the #1 international best seller *Go the Fuck to Sleep,* as well as the novels *Rage Is Back, Angry Black White Boy, The Dead Run,* and *The End of the Jews,* winner of the California Book Award. He has written for the *New Yorker,* the *New York Times, Esquire,* the *Believer,* and National Public Radio's *All Things Considered.* His daughter Vivien is six.

www.AdamMansbach.com

Owen Brozman has illustrated for *National Geographic, Time Out New York,* Scholastic, Ninja Tune, Definitive Jux, and numerous other clients. He and Mansbach's previous collaboration is the acclaimed graphic novel *Nature of the Beast,* and his work has been recognized by the Society of Illustrators of Los Angeles, *Creative Quarterly* journal, *3x3* magazine, and many more. He lives in Brooklyn, New York, with his wife and daughter, whose favorite food is bananas.

www.OwenBrozman.com

For Vivien and Olivia

The sunrise is golden and lovely,
The birds chirp and twitter and tweet,
You woke me and asked for some breakfast,
So why the fuck won't you eat?

The bunnies are munching on carrots,
The lambs nibble grasses and bleat.
I know you're too hungry to reason with but
You have to fucking eat.

Your cute little tummy is rumbling
And pancakes are your favorite treat.
I'm kind of surprised that you suddenly hate them.
That's bullshit. Stop lying and eat.

The giraffes pluck the tender young leaves up,
The mice snack on seeds and on wheat.
No, sweetheart, I can't make spaghetti,
The fucking meal's served. Time to eat.

If we were both pandas I'd know what to feed you,
But seafood is scary, we're leery of meat.
Half the food at the market is probably toxic,
But fuck it, you still have to eat.

You're not finished, and no, you can't go to school
In pajamas, a hat, and bare feet.
Whatever, put shoes on and bring me your plate,
My whole diet's the shit you won't eat.

The sloth and the lemur, the chipmunk and cheetah,
The slow and the sleek and the fleet
Share one thing, my love: they make less of a mess
Than you fucking do when they eat.

How was school, hon? Whoa, your lunch box is full.
How are you not passed out in the street?
How is it you're smart? How the hell are you growing
When you basically don't fucking eat?

You know who loves dinner? The duck-billed platypus.
But I know I'm facing defeat.
This spoon-feeding shit makes me wonder
Why the fuck we weaned you from the teat.

I hope you know it's super-special
To go to a restau— Hey, back in your seat.
You shitting me? This whole menu's crap to you
But a roll on the floor—*that* you'll eat?

Yum, this looks great. Five big bites, my darling.
Fine. Three, but don't try to cheat.
A lot of kids don't get asparagus,
Show some fucking respect for them. Eat.

Oh, now you're hungry? Tough shit, kitchen's closed.
Have some warm milk. For me a scotch, neat.
Pancakes? Yeah, right. It's bedtime, child,
It's too goddamn late now to eat.

I'm pretty sure that you're malnourished
And scurvied. My failure's complete.
But on the bright side, maybe this is the night
You'll go the fuck to sleep.

The End